Leading Worship

GW00750752

Mark Earey
Team Rector of Morley, West Yorkshire
Formerly Praxis National Education Officer

GROVE BOOKS LIMITED
RIDLEY HALL RD   CAMBRIDGE   CB3 9HU

Contents

The Cover Illustration is by Peter Ashton

Author's Note

There is already a Grove booklet in the Worship Series with the title 'Leading Worship' (No 76, by Colin Buchanan). That booklet is now out of print, and the Group for the Renewal of Worship (GROW) decided that something new was required, rather than a revision of that earlier work. However, as an author and worship leader I am very conscious of building on the foundation laid by that booklet. Some of the insights contained therein have been formative in my own thinking about worship and leading of worship, and key parts of its content are summarized here in the knowledge that not everyone will have access to the earlier work.

For various reasons this booklet has been produced rather more quickly than was at first intended. I am indebted to members of GROW who read and commented on earlier drafts, and in particular to Gilly Myers, Vernon Blackmore, Colin Buchanan, James Steven and Phillip Tovey, who all read a later version and made comments under some considerable time pressure. The remaining oversights and errors are, of course, my own responsibility. The greatest debt is owed to my wife, Alison, who has not only read the draft but has also had to live with the reality of my own leading of worship. To her the booklet is dedicated, with love and thanks.

First Impression April 1999
Second Edition January 2005
ISSN 0144-1728
ISBN 1 85174 400 2

Introduction– The Role of the Leader

1

A Worship Leader is...

John is a Reader in his parish church. To lead evensong this Sunday he has to read (or chant) the minister's part, to announce the hymns and, possibly, to preach a sermon and read the Bible.

Jane is a minister in the Bigtown Methodist Circuit. To lead the service at St Peter's Methodist Church this Sunday she will introduce the hymns and lead extempore prayers at various points in the service to encompass praise, confession, response, intercession and the presentation of the collection. Her primary responsibility is to preach the sermon, and the whole service is geared to this.

Dave is the worship group leader at Anytown Community Vineyard Fellowship. To lead the worship he will co-ordinate the musicians and singers and provide some sort of link between the songs. His selection of songs moves from triumphant praise, through gentle adoration to intimate encounter, and prepares the way for a long sermon by the pastor and a time of 'ministry.' Members of the congregation may share prophecies and he will have to respond and possibly change his planned songs to pick up on a new sense of direction or a different emphasis.

Much depends on what is expected of the act of worship and of the leader

Ruth is the Vicar of St Agnes' church. She is presiding at the monthly evening Communion service. To lead the service she says most of the leader's words (including the Eucharistic Prayer) and introduces hymns and songs. She suggests times of silence, and makes sure everyone else who is taking part knows what they are doing and is ready to do it. As the preacher majored on healing, she decides to omit the creed and move straight into a set of responsive intercessions on the theme of healing. She also feels it would be appropriate to provide prayer for healing during the distribution of communion and so during the peace she discreetly asks one or two people to help with this, and tells the congregation before announcing the offertory hymn.

Leading and Planning

The question, 'How can I lead worship well?' is not easy to answer. As the above examples illustrate, much depends on what is expected of the act of worship and of the leader.

In most churches leading worship increasingly means putting a lot of yourself into the process: taking more decisions 'on the hoof,' 'steering'[1] the act of worship itself and 'presiding' over the meeting in such a way as to enable others to play their part and use their gifts. This is partly due to the rediscovery that 'ministry' is something done by the whole people of God, not just the 'minister.' It is also related to Western culture, which increasingly expects greater informality in all walks of life and values spontaneity, associating this with sincerity. I think this is in large part due to the impact of television, where large numbers of people are addressed in an intimate and informal way. Spontaneity (even if it is 'planned spontaneity') is taken as a sign of sincerity and reality. On the television news a 'live' report is valued, even if the reporter can tell us no more than someone sitting in the studio. It is the little asides and jokes between presenters that reassure us that they are normal human beings and lead us to trust them.

The question, 'How can I lead worship well?' is not easy to answer

Because Christians know that God seeks worship 'in Spirit and in truth' (John 4.23f) this has led, in some circles, to an assumption that the Spirit is more active in spontaneous leadership than leadership which includes advance planning.

This booklet is about leading worship. However, leading worship usually involves planning or preparing worship to some degree and so a good deal of space is devoted to planning as well as leading.

Presiding and Pastoring

In liturgical circles the leader of a Communion service is likely to be called the 'president' or 'presider.' This concept of presidency can also be applied to non-eucharistic services. The presiding minister is the person who 'holds the thing together' and with whom the buck stops.

However, leading worship does not happen in a vacuum. Often the regular leader of worship is also the church's main pastor. The development of the early church's worship from primarily domestic gatherings suggests that this has been the case from the earliest days:

> When we recall that the officers of the church were certainly pastors, and presumably led worship because they were pastors, then we see a close ideological connection between pastoring and what we are now beginning to call 'presidency.' To preside at a meeting was an expression of pastoral care…the oversight of worship meetings is an expression of oversight of the people themselves.[2]

Of course, it is not true that the *only* leaders of worship are the pastors of the church, but the pastoral link remains. It is this sense that those who *regularly* lead worship should have some knowledge of the congregation that makes the use of 'outside' clergy to lead services when a church is without a minister seem acceptable as a temporary measure, but not as a permanent feature. Ordained (or other full-time) leaders will usually combine a pastoral ministry with the leading of worship, but *all* worship leaders need to recognize that their leading will have pastoral consequences (for good or ill!) and is exercised in the context of real people and their lives. The leader of worship who never has to wrestle with the complex and sometimes messy realities of supporting members of the church family in their daily lives may have a somewhat two-dimensional approach to the leading of worship.

All worship leaders need to recognize that their leading will have pastoral consequences

Much of this booklet is written on the assumption that one person will act as leader of a given act of worship. However, it is worth reminding ourselves that worship is a corporate act of a community of people, and that the leadership of that worship should also express and emerge out of that community. Leading worship should not be a solitary pursuit. Our integrity as worship leaders will depend on having good relationships with members of the congregation and will be deepened by collaborative patterns of leadership and the expression of appreciation and gratitude to others.

Our integrity as worship leaders will depend on having good relationships with members of the congregation

Clearly this raises particular issues for those who are called on to lead worship 'away' from their normal congregation. It will be important to establish some sort of pastoral relationship with at least some of the congregation before the service. In practice this may be little more than a phone call in advance, greeting a few people as they arrive and taking time with the local 'team' immediately before the service to check the detail of their 'normal' practice. It is not much—but it is a start.

2   Doing Some Groundwork

Understanding the Context

Leading worship in an unfamiliar congregation (as lay preachers and Anglican Readers often do) focuses the mind very effectively in preparation: you cannot take anything for granted. But even leading worship in a familiar church can benefit from a step backwards to examine the context in which the act of worship will take place. For instance:

Even leading worship in a familiar church can benefit from a step backwards to examine the context

- *The global context.* What is happening in the world that will affect the worship this week? An obvious example would be something such as the death of Diana, Princess of Wales, or the Dunblane tragedy. World events will not necessarily dominate the act of worship, but the leader who fails to acknowledge these events gives the impression that worship is unconnected with the rest of life.

- *The community context.* What is happening in the life of the community which will affect the way worshippers approach worship? This might include such things as recent large-scale redundancies in the area.

- *The church context.* What is happening in the life of the church? Has a key church member recently died, or is everybody conscious of a church family coping with a particularly difficult situation at the moment?

- *The worship context.* What sort of service is this, at what time of day and how many people will be there? What is the likely age profile of worshippers and how does the size of the worship space compare with the size of the congregation (are we going to be rattling around a huge building, or squashed into someone's living room)? What are the possibilities for movement and action and what are the 'built-in' symbolic elements of this building? All of these questions and more will affect the way the service is led.

Great Expectations?

One of the key reasons to consider all the above questions is to get a clear sense of the expectations of the worshippers.

- Will they be expecting something fresh and radical, or stable and familiar?

- What level of formality or informality will they expect?

- Will they expect to have a book (if so, which one/s) or printed sheet in their hands, or will they want everything on the screen?

- How long will they expect the service to last?

- How much will they expect to participate actively and how much space and time will they want to reflect quietly?

Of course, understanding expectations is only half of the picture. The next question to consider is whether you intend to work *with* those expectations, or to *challenge* them. Either way, understanding should come first. If you intend to challenge them, then you need to be sure that you are the person with the authority to take that decision. It may be wise to consult with other church leaders if you intend doing something very radically different. Which brings us to the next point…

The next question to consider is whether you intend to work with those expectations, or to challenge them

By What Authority?

All churches have levels of authority, even if they decide differently which things belong at which level. For instance, in the Roman Catholic Church the decision about which Scripture readings to have on a given day is taken at a global level (using a lectionary), whereas in a Baptist church it is likely to be determined by the preacher.

The key question for the worship leader or planner is, 'Who has the right to decide this?' The issue might be as simple as 'What songs shall we sing?' or as potentially complicated as 'Would it be all right to change the wording of the Lord's Prayer to "Our Mother in heaven…"?'? The two scales on which these decisions fall are the Local vs Universal (is this determined by me, by our congregation or by some authority beyond us) and the Temporary vs Regular (I might be able to do this as a once-off, but if it is to be part of our regular pattern I will need to discuss it with the church council).[3]

Give the Worship Away

There seems to be a tendency for worship leaders in all denominations to end up doing and controlling everything themselves. On the whole it seems that the less well prepared the leader is, the more likely the service is to degenerate into a monologue. This is the point at which to examine patterns of worship leading and preparation. If the normal pattern is for one person to plan and lead, then maybe it is time to consider how the planning and leading could be done collaboratively. Acts of worship that are prepared by several people working together are more likely to draw upon the gifts of more than one person when it comes to leading the parts of the service. This will need more advance planning, but it does not necessarily involve complicated structures or more meetings. Simple acts of communication between worship leaders, children's leaders, stewards, and musicians which are built in to normal patterns of planning and leading can go a long way.

It seems that the less well prepared the leader is, the more likely the service is to degenerate into a monologue

And do not restrict the corporate pattern to planning and leading. Make sure you use songs, spoken responses, corporate speaking, corporate actions and familiar words to make the worship feel as if it belongs to all the worshippers and not just to the leader or leaders.

Putting a Service Together 3

Let us begin to think about the process of planning an act of worship.

The material in boxes (below) will give suggestions for how to go about this. Regular leaders of worship will not have time to go through this process in detail every time they lead worship, but it may be a good starting point for those new to leading worship and form a useful framework to which to return.

What Do We Think We Are Doing?

If only Jesus had given us a basic order of service for Christian worship! Most of our problems with worship stem from the fact that he did not. For all the right reasons we want our worship to be 'proper,' to be what God wants and, if we are honest, to be fairly close to the way we like it.

The lack of a blueprint from Jesus (or even Paul) means that we have to think for ourselves. There are lots of aspects of worship (which is why it is such a difficult thing to define); all of them are important and each of us tends to emphasize one aspect over the others. The first hurdle is, therefore, to acknowledge that each of us has a working model in our head of what we think worship should be like. If we are leaders of worship then we are likely to try to form the worship in that image. If that working model is not the same as that of the worshippers then there is likely to be trouble—one way or another it will end in tears (and not necessarily theirs!). I have written elsewhere about some of the different models of worship current in the church today.[4] Suffice it to say that before we go any further in thinking about how to lead worship well, it is essential to stop and do some thinking about what it is that you think you are going to lead, and what it will mean to do it 'well.' There is a world of difference between setting out to lead a powerful emotional encounter with the Spirit of God and trying to lead an edifying encounter with the Word of God (though the results in people's lives the rest of the week should not necessarily be so different). Think of this as a sort of 'leadership audit.'[5]

> *The first hurdle is to acknowledge that each of us has a working model in our head of what we think worship should be like*

Take a minute to try to write down in one sentence your definition of 'worship.' Then try to list some of the implications of this definition as it applies to the practical task of planning and leading a service.

Getting a Sense of Direction

For the person planning and leading an act of worship, the whole thing can sometimes seem like a rather complicated jigsaw, in which all the pieces must be fitted together somehow (preferably in not much more than an hour).

It is more helpful to see a service as a journey, which has a beginning and an ending, and where the two are not the same place! In other words, we must go somewhere. We have come to an 'event' — an event in which we do some business with God that may result in change in our lives either immediately or in the future. It is an event in which we are all participants and in which we find our bearings again in the midst of God's people and in the great story of salvation in which we, in our place and at this time, are only part of something much bigger.

No journey is ever repeated exactly. The route may be the same, but the time, the other passengers, the weather and my mood may all be different. Similarly, no act of worship can be an exact replica of another. The liturgy or the song list may be the same but the people will be different — either a different set of people, or the same people at a different stage in their lives, even if the last service was only a week ago. The leader's task is to know both travellers and route.

It has become common to see each service as needing a theme. A theme can give a sense of coherence to a service, but 'theme' is a static model and can be very constraining. To move beyond a thematic captivity to a sense of direction requires a bigger vision, where the aim is not 'to make everything fit the theme' but is focussed on the result in the lives of the worshippers. Of course, leaders can never enforce a 'result' on the lives of worshippers, but a sense of direction is more likely to make an act of worship a catalyst for growth and change.

Seeing the service as journey with a direction means paying attention to the various modes of transport (the elements), the key places en route (the high-points) and the connections (the transitions).

> Thinking about the service you are planning, try to complete this sentence: I would love the worshippers to leave the service more…

Structure and Shape

A basic understanding of shape and structure in worship is one of the keys (if not *the* key) to good worship leading. The rediscovery of this is one of the results of the C20th 'liturgical movement.' It has led to a remarkable convergence among the 'liturgical' churches in the shape of their services. One has only to experience a post-Vatican 2 Roman Catholic Mass, a Methodist service of the Lord's Supper and a Church of England Common Worship Order One Communion service to see just how close we have come. There is certainly a similarity in the words we use, but what is more remarkable is the shape of what we do. There are some differences of course, but the basic order in which the key elements of the service come, and the clarity with which the structure of the service can be seen are signs of this convergence.

I was in France recently (for work, you understand) staying at a Roman Catholic retreat centre. I was invited to attend Mass at the centre. The service was entirely in French, but it was easy to tell where we were in the service because the basic shape was not only familiar, but was also abundantly clear from such things as symbol, movement and music.

In the Church of England all the Common Worship services begin with a page which gives a basic outline of the service, showing the key elements, the order in which they come and their relative importance. The theory is that if leaders can grasp the essential shape and flow of the service, they are more likely to make sensible choices when they have options, and less likely to cut out the important bits when time is short.

The key to understanding structure is to see it as scaffolding—it is not the end, it is a means. The end is something far more significant. One might define it as 'encountering God' or 'offering ourselves to God' or something similar, depending on what you think worship is all about (see above)—whatever it is, the scaffolding exists simply as a way of making it happen. I think of it as being like decorating a house. To gain access to those tricky places like ceilings, guttering, window frames and so on you need to use a ladder or scaffolding. Liturgy (which I take to mean public, structured worship, determined at least partly translocally) is designed to do the scaffolding job. It tries to give structured access to the immensity of God and to prevent local leaders simply doing their favourite things their way. However, it can seem like overkill when all you want to do is change the lamp shade. Non-liturgical worship is like using a ladder. It has the advantage of flexibility, but constantly moving a ladder is a drag, and so the temptation is to leave it where it is. This means that the parts of the job within easy reach get done really well, and those that are a bit of a stretch get done…less well. The discernment comes in knowing when to use the scaffolding and when to nip in with a ladder.

Sometimes the structure is given to us, either by custom or by rules. For instance, the Communion service has a basic threefold structure of: Word — Prayers — Meal. You could decide to have the bread and wine first and then the Bible readings and sermon (and I know of churches which have done it that way), but it would feel a bit strange, and you would need to have a good reason for doing it.

The tendency in non-eucharistic Sunday worship in many churches is towards an outline structure, into which resource material may be fitted as appropriate.[6] Sometimes the structure is not given to us. This might be the case in an informal celebration meeting, or a time of worship in a house group, either of which could be structured in a number of different ways.

> What is the basic structure of the act of worship you are going to lead? Is it 'given' or will it be locally determined, or a mixture of both? Perhaps the structure will only become clear when you have considered some of the other aspects of the service.

Elements

These are the basic building blocks for worship. Like structure, the elements of a service are sometimes 'given' and sometimes determined by the leader and/or planners. For instance, in a Church of England service of Holy Communion, the basic elements are fixed — there must normally be a penitential section, Bible readings, a sermon, prayers of intercession, an authorized Eucharistic Prayer and so on — but there is some scope for flexibility and an element of choice. (Though not much choice in a *Book of Common Prayer* Communion Service!) Similarly, *A Service of the Word* gives a basic set of elements that ought to be present in any Church of England non-eucharistic service, such as an all age or 'family' service, or an informal evening service. *A Service of the Word* gives a lot of scope, and does not specify the order of the elements, but it does give a basic list against which to test the contents of a Church of England service.

For other denominations the situation is different. In some churches the rules are tighter, in others the elements are determined almost entirely by the leader and local custom. In the latter situation it can be helpful to determine your own checklist of essential elements. This might include such things as penitential material, some prayers, Bible reading(s), sermon, prayers of intercession, some credal or doctrinal material and some element of thanksgiving.

Either nationally or locally determined 'checklists' can usefully be supplemented with other guidelines—a sort of 'contents' checklist: praise, adoration, confession, victory, suffering, compassion, holiness and so on, against which to check a list of songs, the content of a service, or the acts of worship spanning a six month period. This sort of balance ensures that over time the whole truth about God is celebrated in worship. In churches which give some sort of structure to the church year much of this happens naturally over the course of a year.

You might similarly want to check for a balance of spoken and sung, passive and active, silence and noise, action and reflection and so on.

This is the hard long-term work of planning and leading worship. It is not as glamorous as standing at the front preaching or strumming a guitar, but it is just as vital. Worship *forms* our faith (as individuals and as communities) as well as *expressing* our faith. Over time our assumptions and beliefs about God are formed not just by sermons but by the songs we sing, the ways we address God, the things we ask him for and the focus of our liturgy. Leaders of worship have a responsibility to ensure that in the long term God's people are nourished in their worship by the whole truth about God and his kingdom. That means taking the bigger perspective than this Sunday's service.

> Make a list of all the elements to be included in the service. This would include all the necessary elements (those necessary because of the nature of the service or church rules) and all the extras such as notices, banns of marriage, singing happy birthday to someone, a special anthem sung by the choir, and so on.
>
> Mark any elements that could or should include the opportunity to respond in some way, and consider what that response could be.[7]

High-points

The French Mass that I mentioned above was a classic example of how to highlight the really important things in a service. They did it with music. It was a simple Mass, and the only singing was in two places: the acclamation before the reading of the Gospel, and parts of the Eucharistic Prayer. The singing was unaccompanied and simple, but it made the point: two key parts of this service are the Word (with a focus on the gospel) and the Sacrament (with a focus on giving thanks over bread and wine in remembrance of Christ).

In any act of worship it should be clear what the climax is and what the high-points are along the way. Sometimes the climax will come at the end, though it is rare for it to come *right* at the end—you normally need something to 'bring things down to earth' gently again.

A service may have several key elements: gathering, word, prayers, baptism, communion, dismissal and so on. These elements might be emphasized by music, movement, pace, volume, lighting or whatever is appropriate. Of these key structural elements, one or two should dominate as the high-points of the service. The thing to avoid is high-points being completely overshadowed by less important elements.

Go back to your list of elements and put a ring round the one or two most important parts of the service (be ruthless). Now underline any other parts that are key to the structure and flow of the service, but not as important as the ringed elements.

Now consider how you will use music, movement, symbol, smell, lighting or other means to emphasize the high-points and other key elements.

Transitions

Those who lead informal (and especially charismatic) worship are very experienced at handling transitions. The songs move effortlessly from one to the next, sometimes with silence or some instrumental music in between, sometimes with a few words from the leader or perhaps some contributions from the congregation. Often words are projected using an overhead projector, so that books and song numbers are not necessary. Worshippers may be invited to sit or stand as they choose, obviating the need for instructions about posture. When it is done well it is glorious. Of course, it is not always quite like that—but the aim is to help worshippers keep their attention on God rather than on the mechanics of the act of worship. Hymn boards and printed orders of service can achieve a similar flow, but without the same flexibility.

Sometimes liturgical worship seems to lurch from one element to the next. Perhaps this is because leaders are so keen to get the elements right that they forget to consider the transitions.

> Make a list of methods of transition. This might include such things as: silence, informal comment, movement to a different place, music, change of posture or different lighting.

Using Music

Not every service will include music, but when it is used it forms a powerful part of the act of worship and it tends to be used in different ways in different churches. For the sake of argument, perhaps we could caricature the approaches as follows:[8]

> - *Hymns in the gaps.* This is a typical Church of England pattern, where the core service structure is given by the liturgy and the hymns or songs fit into the gaps. The singing is largely used for *transitions*.
> - *Liturgy in the gaps.* This is the classic Free Church model. The core of a service structure consists of several hymns or songs, and any liturgy, prayer, or readings fit in between them. The hymns are key *elements*.
> - *No gaps.* This would be a typical New Church pattern where the songs are the liturgy (or the nearest thing to it). In other words the songs have to do the work of praise, penitence, belief etc and the *structural work* of moving the worship forward, which in liturgical churches is often done by the liturgy.
> - *Making the liturgy sing.* This is a common Roman Catholic pattern (followed also in many Church of England congregations), where some of the words of the service itself are sung (as well as additional songs and hymns).

Music is important in worship because it is a way of connecting our emotional and intellectual responses. This is why the songs or hymns during the distribution of communion are often very important to the congregation. The songs help them feel that they have 'made contact' with God at a point where the liturgy is *speaking* of all that God has given us. A closer integration of music, words and action should result in a closer integration of head and heart, which can only be a good thing if we are to worship with all our mind, soul, heart and strength. The result does not have to be a 'sung liturgy' — it might mean a closer integration of song and confession so that the two are interwoven, or the use of a hymn as a response to the sermon.

There is no rule that says that hymns have to be sung all in one go. Perhaps a verse or two before and a verse or two after the intercessions would be a helpful preparation and conclusion? Or perhaps you could use the verses of a hymn as the structure for confession, with words spoken in between verses? The chorus of a song might make a good repeating response during the Eucharistic Prayer or the intercessions?

Take a look at your service plan so far. How have you used music? Is there any way of using music more creatively so as to integrate emotional and intellectual elements of the worship? Consider particularly the use of song as part of any 'response' sections.

Putting it All Together

Now put the whole thing together in such a way that the structure matches the content and leads smoothly in your chosen direction, emphasizing the key points and making room for response where appropriate.

Do not forget to check the practicalities. How will people know what is happening next? Will you have to announce things, is there a book to use, do you need to print anything on paper or prepare things for the OHP or data projector? What will be the appropriate posture to suggest for each element? Are there people you need to liaise with now or later (musicians, readers, children's leaders, stewards and so on)?

Laying Some
Personal Foundations

4

Be a Servant

It is not easy to combine servanthood and leadership—a point that Jesus' closest friends also grasped. Worship leaders often tend to one of two extremes. They are either totally dominating, or they are so shy of giving a clear lead that they are ineffective. Leadership is a gift from God, given for the benefit of the body. The leader serves by leading well.[9] To serve in leadership is to give more attention to the act of worship as a whole than to one's own part in it, or enjoyment of it. The leader's chief role is to ensure that God is the focus and that others are enabled to use their gifts and play their part.

Liturgy (the corporate, public, worship of the church) is the 'work of the people.'[10] This means that the worship must be owned by the worshippers and the leader must respect the expectations of the worshippers. This is not to say that the congregation must never be challenged, or that nothing must ever change. What it does suggest is that the leader who changes things for the sake of his or her interests or preferences, without consultation and without regard to the wider church does violence to this principle. The increasing flexibility and variety of Church of England liturgy, for instance, brings with it great opportunities, but also carries the danger of clergy spending hours each week tinkering with the liturgy, searching for new texts and imposing them on a defenceless congregation week after week. Any sense of continuity in worship is subsumed by the desire for something new, and the worship becomes the property of the leader alone. The person who controls the photocopier (or computer, or OHP) controls the liturgy.

Colin Buchanan, in his earlier booklet, suggests the model of the meeting with its 'chair' as a helpful way of understanding the relationship between the leader, the worshippers and the act of worship:

> The chairman [sic] has authority—he may speak to articulate the mind of the meeting, or he may intervene to bring the meeting to order. But in general his authority is expressed in helping the meeting follow its anticipated agenda with a minimum of fuss or disruption…He knows who has the major contribution to offer under each heading, and he fulfils his own role by ensuring that each is able to make his contribution in turn in this way…And if something unexpected occurs, then

the flexibility of the chair is able to adapt to it, and bring it within the onward flow of the meeting—so that even a distraction is turned to the benefit of the meeting.'[11]

Be a Worshipper

Learning to worship while you are leading worship can be hard. For most of us, our expectations of worship are so tied up with our own emotional needs, expression and fulfilment, that anything that gets in the way (such as having to consider what is coming next) feels like a hindrance.

The truth is that you cannot worship in the *same* way when you are leading, but that does not mean you cannot worship. It simply means that you have to learn to see the act of leading itself as part of your offering to God. Over time it becomes easier to be less distracted by the practicalities, less nervous and more confident. But always the leader of worship is there primarily as the servant of the worshipping community, and that means an offering to the Lord of a different sort. Do not feel guilty about it.[12]

Understand Your Personality

Personality indicators, such as the Myers-Briggs Type Indicator, are becoming widely used in the church and in the wider world to help people to understand themselves and others.[13] But complicated psychological tools are not essential, though they can be enormously helpful starting points. What is essential is some awareness of the importance of personality in worship. Every person in the congregation will have natural preferences, related to their personality rather than their theology, in the way they like worship to be, and *so will you* as the worship leader!

Worship can never be about trying to keep most of the people happy most of the time. Indeed, I would argue that worship should be a place where we feel safe to be stretched and challenged to discover the parts of our personalities with which we are *not* so familiar or comfortable. However, it is most important that we know ourselves and our own preferences, both to ensure that we do not unconsciously impose our preferred way of doing things on others, and so that we will be aware of those aspects of worship leading that we will find naturally most difficult. This might be formality and structure for one person and open-ended spontaneity for another. Some will naturally tend to services full of silence and reflection; others will find it easier to think of symbols and action to form part of a service. Knowing our own strengths and weaknesses will make us more aware of when we need the help of someone who works differently to us, or when we are going to be leading from a position of particular personal weakness.

Getting Down to the Nitty-Gritty[14] 5

When it comes to worship leading everyone has their own pet hates and their own blind spots.

What follows is a list of some very basic things to get right. Naturally this will reflect my pet hates and my blind spots. You will probably disagree with at least part of it. I am not trying to give a list of liturgical rights and wrongs, but to draw attention to some key areas. Take with a large pinch of salt and apply to your own situation.

Make Sure You Lead 'To Scale'

This simply means getting your leadership right for the size of building, the type of service and the number of people. It affects a whole range of things, such as volume and tone of voice, use of gestures, level of formality, how many procedural announcements to give, the use of humour and what you wear (see also below).

What Do You Look Like?

I have heard people complain about worship leaders wearing each of the following (though not at the same time): brown shoes with a black cassock; skin tight lycra leggings (worn by a woman); skin tight leather trousers (worn by a man); jeans; shorts; a three-piece suit; and vestments that last saw an iron when Graham Kendrick was a new songwriter.

Whether you see these as universal rules of worship leadership or someone's hang-ups depends on whether they are your views or someone else's! I suggest two basic principles when considering dress for leading worship:[15]

1 Try to dress for unity, not to make a point. You may feel that wearing your new Mickey Mouse tie speaks of your freedom from stuffy formalism, but if it speaks to half the congregation of a lack of respect for God and a trivial approach to worship, then your leadership will serve to divide the congregation and draw attention to you—and that is before you have said anything. In some churches the issue will be about whether to wear special robes or vestments

to lead worship. In other places the issue will be what sort of robes or vestments. There are still deeply held views that certain forms of dress necessarily indicate certain doctrinal standpoints.[16]

2 Dress to scale and to context. An impressive gold cope may be right in a packed Carol Service in a large church building—it will definitely not suit an informal agape in a small chapel. Jeans and sweatshirt may suit a Communion service at the end of a Youth Group weekend away, but will not necessarily be right for the Parish Eucharist back home.

Whatever you choose (if the choice is yours), what you wear will probably create the first impression on the congregation, and you want that impression to open the door to worship, not close it. And do not forget that clothes are only part of the battle. The congregation will watch your facial expressions and body language—so try not to look bored!

Be Seen

Being a servant should not mean being invisible. The need for the leader to be heard is an obvious point, but the need to be seen is equally important. The triple-decker pulpit had its drawbacks, but there were some advantages too!

The first need is for clarity about who the presiding minister or overall leader is. In some churches this will be shown by vesture (cassock and surplice, a chasuble, or a dark suit). Sometimes it is indicated by position (who gets to sit on the platform, in the vicar's stall or on the biggest chair) or by some other means, such as who wears the radio microphone. The important thing is that one way or another it is clear who is in charge. This may include introducing yourself, if not everyone will know who you are. This is not for reasons of power or status, but simply so that the congregation can see that someone is in control of the service so that everyone else can focus on God. Being visible is also important so that the leader can give visual clues as to what is happening. Visitors in particular will instinctively look at the leader to see what to do.

The important thing is that one way or another it is clear who is in charge

This is increasingly an issue where several people share the leading of a service. In a positive scenario, this would be because one person is presiding over the whole event, but is appropriately delegating elements within the service to others. In a less idealistic scenario the first part of a Communion service may be led by a Reader or other lay leader, with the vicar arriving breathless during the peace, hotfoot from a service elsewhere. Whatever the situation, whenever leadership is handed over it is important that it is done clearly and positively, so that everyone knows who is now taking the lead.

Learn the Art of Invitation

There is a very important distinction between inviting and commanding. The former gives a clear lead and yet still gives people permission to opt out. This is particularly important if the congregation includes visitors who are not used to church. The aim should be to put people at ease, not to put them on the spot. Most visitors will not mind what whacky things the congregation gets up to as long *as they do not necessarily have to do the same.*

Beginnings

Some churches mark the beginning by the entrance of a procession, the start of the first hymn, or the turning on of the overhead projector. Whatever you do, make it clear. There is nothing wrong with some silence before a service, or some music or worship songs to help people prepare themselves, but everyone needs to know when we have stopped being a collection of individuals and are being summoned as a *body* of people to worship God together. In other words, people need to know when the chatting should stop.

The opening greeting will establish a relationship between leader and the rest of the congregation

The opening greeting will establish a relationship between leader and the rest of the congregation. Everyone has a preference, but the key thing is to use a greeting that is right for the context, and to remember that greetings convey unspoken messages:

- 'Hello!' ('Good morning,' 'Welcome everyone,' etc) is a reflection of shared human ordinariness that links worship with the rest of life.

- 'The Lord be with you—And also with you,' speaks of shared prayer for one another and an expectation of God's presence.

- A sentence of Scripture as the first utterance puts the emphasis firmly on God, but does not establish a relationship between worshippers.

- 'I couldn't hear you singing,' establishes a (probably unhealthy) relationship of power.

Endings

Colin Buchanan once wrote, 'I assert as a matter of principle that services should only end once.'[17] I suggest one minor amendment to this principle, which is that services may end several times, but should only end once for any individual worshipper. The church of the fourth century knew how to end a service for some, while allowing it to continue for others: they dismissed the catechumens (those preparing for Christian initiation) and continued the service for those who were initiated. Today services often end with a blessing, but there are still people being prayed for, or prayer is offered for those who would value it. Or perhaps a more informal service has gone on for an hour and a half. Some are beginning to look at their watches, but it is clear that others would value the chance to stay longer. The service may need a 'pseudo-ending' to allow those who wish to leave to do so without embarrassment, whilst allowing others to linger longer.

Leading Where Others Must Follow

The leader needs to be clear in giving directions and giving a lead for spoken texts. There are different ways of introducing words that the congregation join in:

- You can say 'We say together...'
- You can start them off with the first line and they join in with the rest.
- You can say the first line yourself as a cue, and they then repeat it and carry on with the rest.
- You can give them a separate 'cue' line.[18]

Separate cue lines require either a printed text with the congregation's words clearly indicated in bold, or a familiar cue line for a particular prayer. Well established examples in the Church of England would include, 'Lord in your mercy,' which will normally elicit the response, 'Hear our prayer,' or, 'As our Saviour taught us, so we pray,' which should produce, 'Our Father...' Whichever method you use, consistency is the name of the game.

The Lord's Prayer is a particularly tricky case. Many churches are now bilingual—they use a traditional form of the Lord's Prayer at some services and a modern form at others. As the form used is not always printed it is vital that leaders make a good clear start in such a way that the congregation know which form to use. If the text is not printed, and there is no 'cue line,' leaders tend to introduce the traditional form like this:

> 'Our Father [slight pause, then everyone joins in:] who art in heaven…'

The modern forms[19] need to be introduced slightly differently:

> 'Our Father in heaven [all said in one breath, then a slight pause, then everyone joins in:] hallowed be your name…'

Once you have launched a congregational text, maintain a clear lead right to the end. Do not fade out halfway through or start getting the next thing ready. The same rules apply to leading a time of silence. Be confident and clear and give a strong lead (do not fidget or get a book ready during silences).

Directions About Posture

If you are suggesting a posture, it is usually best to mention it last: 'Our next hymn is number 7, we stand to sing.' If you do it the other way round the sound of movement will drown out the instruction.

Though the earlier point about 'inviting' rather than 'commanding' applies here, remember that giving total freedom about posture can be equally unhelpful. 'During the next group of songs please stand or sit as you feel you want to,' sounds flexible. In fact such *carte blanche* simply leaves people watching for a brave soul who will take a lead. If there is no brave soul the worship is likely to take place with everyone seated throughout! A better introduction would be, 'During these songs please feel free to sit or stand, but let's stand to sing our first song.' In general it is easier for individuals to choose to sit when everyone starts off standing than the other way round.

We tend to work with standing as the default posture for singing, but sitting may be better for some situations. For instance, if you have a lot of visitors (a civic service, or a baptism perhaps) it will be easier for everyone to remain seated to sing a song which will be unfamiliar to visitors. Somehow it makes you feel less vulnerable if you are not standing. Sitting may also be useful for a song used as a response to God or a time of reflection, such as after the sermon or as part of the prayers.

Humour

Humour can be a great help in 'humanizing' an act of worship and can be useful when things go wrong, but it needs to be used with care. Jokes are often a cover for a lack of confidence, and the wisecracking leader may simply make the congregation feel they are not in safe hands.

Never use asides that only part of the congregation can hear

Never use asides that only part of the congregation can hear, or in-jokes that only part of the congregation will understand. Both will undermine the sense of unity that the leader should be focussing.

Watch Your Language

Worship is more than singing. Try to avoid saying things like, 'After the prayers we'll have a time of worship,' if what you mean is, 'After the prayers we'll spend some time singing quietly.' If you have a group of musicians and singers it may be better to call them the Music Group than the Worship Group.

Movement

In some churches the leader never has to move further than from the microphone to the OHP, but if yours is the sort of church where things are well spaced, and where movement between them is given symbolic significance, then you will need to be able to move properly.

There are all sorts of rules for those that want them about how you should hold your hands and when you should bow and which way you should face, but the only essential rule is to move with purpose and confidence and otherwise to stay still.

The only essential rule is to move with purpose and confidence and otherwise to stay still

Explanations

Helpful explanations about what is happening in a service can be great for helping people to grow in understanding and to participate more actively, whether the explanation is about the use of ash on Ash Wednesday or about singing in tongues. However, worship is not Religious Education, and leaders need to be cautious about saying too much. On the whole it is better to let a symbol speak for itself than to speak for it. All-Age or 'Family' services seem to be particularly vulnerable to the descent of worship into trendy RE.

When It Goes Wrong 6

As a One-off: If something goes wrong during the service, there are several possible responses:

- Own-up, and never cover-up. It is usually best to be completely honest and straightforward if there has been a mistake and it is obvious. You do not need to point out mistakes of which the congregation is unaware.
- Apologise, if necessary (that is, if it is your fault or if you need to take responsibility).
- Use humour, but only if you are sure it is appropriate and if you can do it confidently rather than nervously.

Then make a confident new start.

As a Regular Pattern: So the service felt like a disaster (again). You return home discouraged. How can you help yourself to do better?

- *Get another perspective.* You may feel the service did not go well, but is that how it seemed to others? You may be being over-critical of yourself.
- *Get some prayer support.* Worship leaders need prayer before the services they lead, they need prayerful support during the services (and often they need prayer after the service!).
- *Establish some supportive feedback.* Leaders who work in teams may find it fairly easy to establish regular patterns of evaluation, but all of us need others to help us assess our leadership and improve. Find a few members of the congregation whom you trust and ask them to help you. They will need help to be systematic. Encourage them always to note the good things first. When we are affirmed and valued we find it much easier to receive constructive criticism and suggestions. But remember, leading worship is physically, emotionally and spiritually draining, so ask them never to say critical things about the service straight afterwards, even if their criticisms are constructive. If they wait at least three days before sharing any comments then both you and they will be able to take a more objective look at the service.
- *Face the ultimate challenge—a different ministry.* If you never feel that the services you lead are as they should be, and others tend to agree, then it just might be that God wants you to major on something else.

7 Resources— Where to Go for Further Help

There are lots of books (and booklets!) on liturgy and worship. Many useful ones are referred to in the notes of this booklet. Your church leader may be able to suggest others. A good way to get up to date information or thinking about worship is to browse or ask at your local Christian bookshop.

The following organizations are among those offering courses or publications:

Music and Worship Foundation offers a consultation service, regional events and higher education courses at London School of Theology. For information contact: James Turner, MWF Administrator, The Annexe, Vicarage Lane, Somerton, Somerset TA11 7NQ. Tel: 01458 272295.

Praxis is a Church of England organization for training and education in worship. They have published various books and resources relating to new liturgical material and run an annual programme of events around the country. For programme information and general enquiries, contact Praxis at Cleveland Lodge, Westhumble, Dorking, Surrey RH5 6BW (Tel: 01306 872 829 Email: Praxis@praxisworship.org.uk) Web: http://www.praxisworship.org.uk

Worship Together magazine is published by Kingsway. It includes articles for worship leaders, musicians and pastors. There is also a Worship Together Resource pack and seminar training programme. For more information contact: Kingsway Communications Ltd, Lottbridge Drove, Eastbourne, East Sussex, BN23 6NT, Web: http://www.worship.co.uk

The Royal School of Church Music (RSCM) publishes a quarterly liturgy planner called *Sunday by Sunday*, which gives suggestions for music linked to the three-year lectionary. Tel: 01306 877676. Web: http://www.rscm.com

Worship and Preaching magazine is published quarterly and carries general articles on worship and preaching and worship notes related to the three-year lectionary (RCL). Contact: Methodist Publishing House, 20 Ivatt Way, Peterborough PE3 7PG.

Notes

1 Colin Buchanan has suggested that the gift in 1 Corinthians 12.28 (*kubernesis* = 'steering') usually translated as 'administration' (NIV and RSV) or 'forms of leadership' (NRSV) might mean 'steering worship.' See *Encountering Charismatic Worship* (Grove Ministry and Worship Series booklet W 51) p 22 footnote 2, quoted in *Leading Worship* (Grove Worship booklet W 76) p 5.

2 Colin Buchanan, *Leading Worship* (Grove Worship booklet W 76) p 6. For a similar argument, but starting from the leadership of worship as an argument for pastoring, see Neville Clark, *Pastoral Care in Context* (Rattlesden: Kevin Mayhew, 1992).

3 Anglicans and Roman Catholics will need to take into account any relevant rubrics and canons.

4 'Worship—What do we think we are doing?' in Evangel, Vol 16, No 1, Spring 1998, pp 7–13.

5 See my *Worship Audit* (Grove Worship booklet W 133) for some thoughts about how a local church can set about examining their assumptions about worship, and evaluating what they do in that light.

6 Church of England non-eucharistic worship (other than BCP services) is covered by *A Service of the Word* as found in the Common Worship main volume page 21ff and *New Patterns for Worship* (London: CHP, 2002) page 9ff. This allows for a variety of structures and specifies key elements of a service, but the content can be drawn from a number of sources. See Trevor Lloyd, *A Service of the Word* (Grove Worship booklet W 151). *The Methodist Worship Book* (Peterborough: Methodist Publishing House, 1999) prints two basic orders for morning or evening worship sharing a common fourfold structure but developed in slightly different ways. Additional resource material is suggested and provided.

7 For some ideas about ways of encouraging a response to the sermon, see John Leach, *Responding to Preaching* (Grove Worship booklet W 139).

8 I owe much of the following to John Leach.

9 A point made by the apostle Paul in Romans 12.8.

10 This is the meaning of the Greek word *leitourgia*, which occurs in various forms in the New Testament, usually translated as 'ministering' (eg Acts 13.2) and

which was used in the Greek translation of the Old Testament to refer to the public sacrificial worship.

11 Colin Buchanan, *Leading Worship*, pp 7f.

12 I have written elsewhere about the model of worship as a drama, where the leader is one of the leading characters, who has to stay 'in role' for the sake of the other actors (*Worship as Drama*, Grove Worship booklet W 140).

13 See Robert Innes, *Personality Indicators and the Spiritual Life* (Grove Spirituality booklet S 57) for a helpful look at the positives and negatives of these tools, with special reference to the Myers-Briggs Type Indicator and the Enneagram.

14 Further practical advice about leading worship can be found in *Worship as Drama* (Grove Worship booklet W 140). For a useful guide to the appropriate use of different sorts of music, see John Leach's *Hymns and Spiritual Songs* (Grove Worship booklet W 132). There is also practical advice in his *Living Liturgy* (Eastbourne: Kingsway, 1997) especially chapters 7, 8 and 9.

15 Dick Hines has written further about the whole issue of what you wear to lead worship in his *Dressing for Worship* (Grove Worship booklet W 138).

16 Canon B 8 states that the Church of England 'does not attach any *particular* doctrinal significance to the diversities of vesture permitted…' (emphasis mine).

17 *Leading Worship*, p 19.

18 There is more about this in John Leach, *Living Liturgy* (Eastbourne: Kingsway, 1997) pp 165ff.

19 I say 'forms' because the decision by the Church of England to continue using the *ASB* modern language Lord's Prayer while most other denominations have chosen the international ecumenical (ELLC) text (with the line, 'Save us from the time of trial…') means that we will have two contenders for the form of the Lord's Prayer to be used in ecumenical gatherings where a modern form is desired.